The Crayfish Catchers

Tom Moorhouse

Illustrated by
Maribel Lechuga

OXFORD
UNIVERSITY PRESS

OXFORD
UNIVERSITY PRESS

Great Clarendon Street, Oxford, OX2 6DP,
United Kingdom

Oxford University Press is a department of the University of Oxford.
It furthers the University's objective of excellence in research, scholarship,
and education by publishing worldwide. Oxford is a registered trade mark of
Oxford University Press in the UK and in certain other countries

Text © Tom Moorhouse 2017

Illustrations © Maribel Lechuga 2017

The moral rights of the author have been asserted

First published 2017

British Library Cataloguing in Publication Data
Data available

978-0-19-837767-2

3 5 7 9 10 8 6 4

Paper used in the production of this book is a natural, recyclable product
made from wood grown in sustainable forests. The manufacturing process
conforms to the environmental regulations of the country of origin.

Printed in China by Golden Cup

Acknowledgements
Inside cover notes written by Becca Heddle
Author photograph by A. L. Harrington Photography

Contents

1 The Race   5

2 Running the Rapids   13

3 Crunching Crayfish   20

4 The Voice in the Waterfall   28

5 The Search for Alder   38

6 The Fight   47

7 The Great River   54

About the author   64

Chapter 1
The Race

Willow stuck her head out of the burrow. She sniffed the air. Nothing. No scent of enemies.

"OK Alder, it's safe," she whispered. "Where's Mother?"

Alder was still in the tunnel. He peered back into the darkness. "I think she's in the nest."

"Brilliant!" Willow grinned at her brother. "We'll be there and back before she knows."

"Come on, then, you're blocking the way," said Alder.

The two water voles ran out into the tall grass of the river bank. In front of them the Great River rippled in the sun. Here the river ran slow, but where they were going she was fast and fun.

"Morning, you big, weedy river!" shouted Willow. "Are you ready to play?"

"You shouldn't talk to her like that," said Alder.

"Who? The river? Why not?"

"You just shouldn't." Alder frowned. "Anyway, are we talking, or racing?"

Willow crouched, ready to run. "We're racing."

"Good." Alder's eyes widened. He stared behind her. "Wait – what's that?"

Willow froze. Had he seen an enemy: a fox, a heron? She glanced back and Alder sprinted off, laughing.

"Hey!" yelled Willow. "Not fair."

The two water voles dashed down the river bank, to the place where the fast water, the rapids, began. They stopped, panting, at the top pool.

"You cheated!" Willow gasped. "I'd definitely have won if you hadn't."

"You never win. Your legs are too little."

"Hah," said Willow. She went down to the water's edge, and cleaned her whiskers. The pool here was wide, dark and smooth. But a little way down was where the white water started. She heard the bubble and splash of the first rapids, and her paws tingled with excitement. This was going to be great.

Alder joined her. "Remember the rules?"

"Of course. We swim together to the edge of the rapids, then we race." She grinned. "And the last one to the bottom's a smelly weasel."

Alder sniffed her. "You're already a smelly weasel."

"Very funny. Ready to go?"

"Shouldn't we say something to the Great River? You know, like Mother does."

Willow sighed. Mother always whispered 'May your waters be kind' to the river before swimming – which was silly because the river was, well, just water. And now Alder had started doing it, too.

"All right, I'll say something." Willow cleared her throat. "Stupid river, you're too slow, can't catch me, I've got to go!"

And she leaped into the water. Alder dived after her, and they came up together.

"I told you not to," he said. "You'll annoy her."

Willow blinked at him. "Annoy who?"

"The river," said Alder.

"Now you're annoying *me*," said Willow. "Come on, let's race."

She paddled towards the rapids, with Alder beside her. The pool was still, and the sun warm. It felt good to be swimming. But ahead of them the calm ended, at the rapids' dark, frothy edge. And that was where the fun began.

"Stay level with me," Alder warned. "We're getting close."

Willow felt the river start to pull. The flow carried them towards the edge of the rapids. The sound of running water grew louder. She glanced at Alder.

"Ready?" she called.

Faster, more urgent, the Great River tugged them onward. The edge of the rapids came closer.

"Ready and steady!" shouted Alder.

And now all they could see was foam and bubbles, and black water that poured between rocks. The river swirled and jostled. The noise became a roar.

"Steady," panted Willow. She was swimming hard. She fought to keep in the centre of the flow, to stay near her brother. "Steady ..."

The river surged. The edge was a vole's length away, then half a length, then:

"Go, go, go!" she yelled.

Willow dived for where the flow was strongest. And the Great River snatched her, and hurled her down into the fury of the rapids.

Chapter 2
Running the Rapids

Water pounded around Willow. It rushed and raced. It surged and plunged. She flowed with it, and it filled her with the thrill of its speed. She glanced over at Alder. He too was grinning with excitement.

"Ha ha!" cried Willow. "It's brilliant! It's great!" She shot down a fall, and bounced up on a swell of water. "This is easy! It's so *easy*!"

"Watch where you're going!" Alder shouted. "There's a wave—"

His next words were lost. Cold water slammed over Willow's head. The river tumbled her and pulled her under. She tried to swim up, to get her nose to the air. But the current dragged her down to where it was black and frightening. Water was in Willow's ears, her eyes, her mouth. She filled with panic. "Which way is up?" she thought. "Which way is up?"

And then Willow saw sunlight glimmering in the water, far above her. *That way!* She kicked out and battled up until she splashed through the surface. She gasped down a breath.

"A – Alder?" she spluttered. "Alder!"

But now he was far away across the river, a tiny shape among the foaming water and black rocks. And Willow could see that he too was struggling.

"Alder!" she yelled. "Alder, are you OK?"

He could not hear her. The Great River was roaring, and the noise was getting louder. Willow spun to face downstream.

"Oh no!"

Ahead of her lay the dark shape of a boulder. Water frothed as it smashed into the rock. It was huge, and Willow was speeding right for it. She clawed desperately at the water, trying to drag herself out of the way. She just managed to twist past the rock, fending it off with her paws. And then it was gone, left behind as she hurtled onward.

"Too close," Willow gasped. "That was too close."

And now the river was full of boulders. Willow dodged and dived, swimming with everything she had.

Her muscles ached. Her breath came hard. But she could not stop, not for an instant – not until the rapids were done. She was nearly at the end, she knew. There was only one more stretch of fast water between her and the calm of the low pool. But it was the most dangerous of all. It was the waterfall.

A new sound rose from the Great River, a low rumble that made Willow's heart thump. Here the river rushed between steep walls of rock. There was no escape, and no way back.

The only way was over the waterfall. Stay where the flow was deepest, time your dive right, and everything would be fine. Willow had done it many times, but now it filled her with fear.

The waterfall's rumble became a snarl, a bellow. The river pounded around Willow.

"Not yet," thought Willow. "Wait. Wait … Now!"

Willow dived, straight into the heart of the Great River. It flung her over the waterfall. She spun in the air, and white water frothed around her. Then she smashed through the surface of the water, down to where it churned. The Great River held her there, far below the surface, for long moments before spitting her out into the calm of the pool.

Willow came up, panting for air. She swam to the grasses by the bank and pulled herself from the river. Then she huddled in the reeds and shivered. She and Alder had raced the rapids many times, but this time it had been different. This time it had frightened her.

Alder's small shape hurtled over the waterfall and shot down, down into the pool. Moments later he bobbed to the surface, paddled to the bank, and climbed out.

"Wow," he panted, "that ... that was scary, wasn't it?"

Chapter 3
Crunching Crayfish

The sight of her brother made Willow feel better. She stood up and brushed some of the water from her fur.

"Don't be such a baby, it wasn't too bad," she said. Her voice shook a bit, so she cleared her throat. "Anyway, I won. What took you so long?"

"I don't know," said Alder, still breathing quickly. "It's never been like that before. I—" He stopped dead. He stared past Willow. "Look," he hissed.

Willow spun. Further down the bank a stranger, a female water vole, was sitting at the water's edge. She held something Willow had never seen before. The object was large, hard-looking and blue-brown. The female raised it to her mouth and bit into it with a crack.

"Hey," squeaked Willow, "who are you?"

The female blinked and turned to face them. Willow stood up taller on her hind legs, ready to fight if the female attacked. The female put her head on one side.

"It's OK, I don't mean you any harm," she said. She watched Willow's face. "I'm sorry I startled you."

Willow dropped down to all fours. "I wasn't startled," she lied.

The female smiled.

"What are you doing here?" asked Alder.

"I like to come here sometimes," said the female. "It's a nice place. It's quiet and there are crayfish."

"Crayfish?" said Willow.

The female held up the blue-brown thing. "This. If you're quick you can sometimes catch one. They're very tasty."

Intrigued, Willow crept forwards. "As tasty as grass?"

"Tastier," said the female, "but much harder to catch." She smiled. "Grass doesn't fight back."

Alder too came closer. Bits of crayfish shell lay all around where the female had been feeding.

"Go ahead," said the female, "try some."

Willow grabbed a bit, then dashed back a safe distance. You shouldn't get too close to strangers, that's what Mother always said. Willow turned the piece of crayfish in her paws. It was hard and blue-brown on one side, red below.

"That's a bit of claw," said the female.
Willow stared. A claw? But it was
huge, the size of her head. Alder peered
over her shoulder.

"I think it's from one of the scuttley things," said Willow. "You know, the big ones with lots of legs on the bottom of the river."

"That's right," said the female, "the scuttley things are crayfish."

"Where do you find them?" said Alder.

"Lots of places, but most of them are back there," the female nodded at the waterfall. "They like the still water behind the falls."

Willow sniffed at the claw. It smelled temptingly of meat. Alder reached in and pulled white flesh from inside. He sniffed it. Then he nibbled, carefully.

"That tastes amazing!" he said.

Willow tried some, too. "It's delicious." She grinned at Alder. "We *have* to get more of this."

The female stopped smiling. "Please don't try. I wouldn't want you to get hurt."

She nodded at the grasses above
them. "You're young. Stick to reed
stems for now. It takes time and skill
to catch crayfish. Like I said, they fight
back." She stood up. "Anyway, I should
go. I've given you enough bad ideas for
one day."

The female turned to leave. Willow
heard Alder gasp.

"What happened to your tail?" he said.

Willow stared. Most of the female's tail was gone. There was only a stump left.

"Did a crayfish do that to you?" asked Willow.

"No," said the female, "it was something bigger. Remember, the Great River is dangerous. Always treat her with respect." She paused. "And please give my regards to your mother. Tell her my name is Fern."

Fern nodded once to Willow and Alder. Then she left, with a rustle of grass.

Alder picked up the crayfish claw. He turned it in his paws.

"Willow," he said, "do you know what I'm thinking?"

"You're thinking 'let's catch a crayfish', aren't you?" said Willow. She frowned. "But Mistress Fern said it's difficult."

"Maybe for others," said Alder, waving a paw. "But we're different. Come on, what do you say?"

Willow put her head on one side. Then she grinned. "What I say is 'yummy'."

And she dived back into the water.

Chapter 4
The Voice
in the Waterfall

There was a splash behind Willow, and Alder paddled up next to her.

"Where do we start?" said Willow.

Alder nodded towards the waterfall. "She said most of the scuttleys are behind the waterfall. So that's where we're going."

Willow watched the water as it pounded down into the pool.

"I can't see a way around the side," she said. "We'll have to swim right under the falls."

Alder grinned at her. "Are you scared?"

"No, of course not," said Willow. But that was not entirely true. There was something about the idea that didn't sound good.

"Then let's do it!" said Alder.

He pushed past Willow and swam off. Willow reluctantly followed. Soon they were bouncing on waves, and swimming hard against the flow.

"How close do we need to get?" Willow shouted. "This is hard work!"

Alder grinned at her. "Let's find out! It's time to dive!"

Willow took a deep breath and dived with Alder, spiralling down through the water. They had to get to the bottom, then push through the churning water beneath the waterfall. But here below the surface the river was dark, and horribly strong. Currents rushed and swirled, forcing them back.

Willow swam as hard as she could, fighting to the place right beneath where the waterfall hit the pool. Bubbles shot down from above, and scattered all around her. Sand and silt whisked up into black clouds that billowed and cleared.

For a moment the clouds parted, and
Willow glimpsed the calm water behind
the waterfall. She saw brown bodies, legs
and claws clustering there. It was full of
crayfish!

Willow smiled, and swam towards the
crayfish. But then a terrible sound rang
in her ears. It was the roar of the river,
almost like a song, almost like words.

"Not you," it seemed to say. "Not you, who insulted me."

And a current caught her and flung her away. It spun her up through the water and shoved her through the surface. Willow gasped with shock.

Alder came up next to her, looking worried.

"Are you OK?" he said.

"No, I'm not," Willow panted. "That was nasty. I – I didn't like it."

"You got caught out by the water, that's all," said Alder.

Willow said nothing. Suddenly, she was really scared. It felt like there was something down there in the water, something that didn't like her.

"Take a deep breath," said Alder, "let's try again."

And before Willow could speak, he dived back down. She stared after him. "It's fine," she thought. "It's only a river. I just have to swim faster, that's all."

She dived, swimming back down to where the current was strongest. She battled all the way to the place where she could see crayfish. But before she could kick through to the still water, the river roared even louder.

"You will not be here!" The voice howled in Willow's mind. "You are unwelcome. Now go!"

Water slammed into her, hard enough to knock the breath from her lungs. It sent her tumbling up and away.

"Argh!" Willow splashed into the air. And this time she did not dare go back down. She swam in the pool, frightened and shivering, until Alder came up next to her.

"I ... I nearly made it that time," he said, between breaths. "I reckon we can do it."

But Willow had had enough.

"I don't want to," she said. "I don't want crayfish."

Alder's eyes narrowed. "Why not?"

"I don't know." Willow felt a chill run through her. "I ... I just didn't like it, that's all."

"That's stupid," said Alder, "we were so close!" His eyes glittered. "I want crayfish and I'm going to get them."

"Then do it on your own," Willow told him. "I'm leaving."

And she swam to the bank and got
out. Alder, though, turned his back and
dived. Long moments later he came up,
dragged down a breath, then dived back
down. Again and again he swam to the
waterfall. But finally, he had to give in,
swim to the side, and pull himself from
the water.

"I can catch one," he said to Willow, "I know I can. But it's like something was stopping me." Alder stared back at the river. "I've got a plan, though. I know exactly how to get to those crayfish."

And now Alder's face frightened Willow even more than the waterfall had. He looked angry. "Alder, please," she said, "we need to stop. We need to go home."

"Why? What's wrong with you?" Alder demanded.

What could Willow tell him? That the Great River hated her, and didn't want her there? That she was afraid to go back? That she was worried that Alder would get hurt?

"I'm cold, and tired, that's what!" said Willow. "And this game is stupid. Now are we going home or what?"

"All right," said Alder. "But we're coming back tomorrow, right?"

Willow didn't answer. She didn't want to come here again. Not tomorrow, not ever. But all she said was, "Come on."

Willow set off up the bank, making for the warm comfort of their burrow. And after a moment Alder reluctantly followed.

Chapter 5
The Search for Alder

Willow woke in the nest. It was early, and her muscles were stiff and achy from the previous day. She wanted to sleep more, but something told her not to. She raised her head and listened. Rain was drumming hard on the soil above her. She felt the space to her side where Alder should be lying, curled next to her. But her paw found nothing. The nest was empty. Alder had gone.

Fear flooded through Willow. She scrambled to her feet.

"Alder?" she hissed.

There was no answer.

"Alder?"

Nothing. And Willow remembered the look she had seen on Alder's face the day before. She remembered how hard he had tried to catch crayfish, and the strange way his eyes had glittered. The memories sent shivers down to her paws. She knew where Alder was, and what he was doing. And she knew that he was in terrible danger.

Willow dashed from the nest. She sprinted through the tunnels and out into the rain. She fled down through the grasses beside the river. In her mind was only one thought: the waterfall, she had to get to the waterfall. She ran past the start of the rapids, past the rocks and boulders, and down, down towards the pool. The Great River had been there all of Willow's life, like the sun, the grass and the earth of the bank. But today, the river looked cold and unfriendly. The rain fell into the water with a constant hiss. To Willow it sounded like a warning. It made her run faster.

Willow stumbled to a stop, right beside the waterfall. Yesterday it had been powerful and dangerous. But now it was swollen with rain. Now it thundered and raged.

"Alder!" Willow cried. "Alder, where are you?"

Willow searched the river, desperately seeking any sign of her brother. She caught sight of a tiny ripple, far above the waterfall. As it rushed closer her paws clenched. It was Alder, racing down the rapids. "So that was his plan to get the crayfish," thought Willow. "He's going down the waterfall first."

"Alder, stop!" Willow cried. "Swim to the side!"

But he did not hear, or was not listening.

"It's not safe! Go back," yelled Willow. "Please go back!"

Faster Alder went, and faster.

Willow could see him struggling. She saw the flow take him, saw him swept over the edge. And then he was gone.

Willow sprinted down to the pool, yelling. "Alder!" she cried. "Alder!"

"What's the matter?" said a voice. "Why are you shouting?"

Willow spun to find the female water vole, Fern, standing in front of her.

"It's Alder, my brother," cried Willow. "He went over the falls. I think he was – he was trying to dive for crayfish."

"I see." Fern frowned at the water. "Not a good day for swimming."

Willow watched, heart thumping, waiting to see some sign, anything to show that Alder was all right. She saw nothing. But in her mind she heard the voice of the Great River. "Mine," the river seemed to say. "I have him. He's mine."

"He's not coming up!" Willow clasped her paws together.

"Something's wrong."

"Give him time," said Fern. "He's young, and strong."

"But can't you hear the river?" The words burst from Willow, almost a sob.

"Can't you hear her voice?"

"The Great River's speaking?" Fern ran up and grabbed Willow's shoulders. "What does she say? Tell me, quickly now."

"She's angry," Willow stammered.
"She's so angry. She – she's taken Alder.
She has him!"

Willow almost expected Fern to laugh.
But Fern did not. Instead, she stared into
Willow's eyes for a moment longer.

"Then you fight!" Fern's grip on
Willow tightened. "Fight with everything
you have. Come on!"

Fern let go and dived for the water.
Willow hesitated, standing on the bank.

"Please," she whispered to the river. "Please let him go. He's my brother."

And a sound rose up from the water. "Then come," it seemed to say. "Come and claim him."

Willow crouched. "I will."

And she dived for the water, swimming as hard as she could.

Chapter 6
The Fight

Fern was strong and quick, but Willow caught up with her easily. Willow's muscles hurt, and she shook with cold and fear, but she ignored all of it. She was here to fight the Great River. She was here to fight for Alder.

"Here," she called to Fern. "This is the place. Come on!"

Willow kicked down below the surface. Swirls spun against her, trying to carry her away, but Willow fought them off. She clenched her jaw and swam faster.

Already, Willow could feel the need to breathe growing in her chest. And Alder had been down even longer. They had to get through the waterfall. They had to get to him soon! Together, Willow and Fern battled beneath the waterfall, right to where the current was strongest.

Willow scanned the water, seeking any sign of Alder. There! There in the calm, beyond the bubbles and the clouds of silt, Willow could see claws waving and snapping. And among them was a larger shape, half hidden in the gloom. It seemed to be struggling and fighting. Willow's heart leaped. It was Alder, she was sure of it. Willow flung herself at the river, scratching and clawing. Fern swam strongly at her side.

But then the water around them turned icy cold. It roared in Willow's ears. "Mine," bellowed the Great River. "He's mine!"

The river surged, trying to push Willow back. But Willow, too, was angry.

"Leave him alone!" Willow yelled in her mind. "Give him back!"

A savage current rushed from nowhere. It crashed against them. In an instant Fern was gone, whirled away. But Willow twisted past the flow, diving around it. She swam and swam, pushing towards Alder. But the Great River matched her, keeping her back. And soon Willow grew tired. Her chest hurt with the urge to breathe. She would have to give in and swim away. But if she did then the Great River had won, and Alder was lost forever.

Willow filled with despair. "Please," she thought. "I'm sorry. I'm so sorry I was rude to you. Please let me through. Please give Alder back. Please!"

The Great River seemed to hesitate. The roar became a growl. The current grew weaker, just for a moment. And Willow, with the last of her strength, thrust and twisted. She burst through the waterfall, and out into the calm beyond.

The water here was clear, and still. The bottom was covered with crayfish, claws raised and snapping. And among them was Alder, still fighting. He was held tight, caught by a crayfish claw that gripped his tail.

Willow plunged to the attack. Crayfish snatched at her legs, her fur, her paws, but she shook them away. She grabbed the claw that held Alder. She pulled it to her face and bit down, hard.

The claw cracked. It opened. And Alder and Willow shot up towards the surface. They burst out into the air, gasping and choking. They breathed deeply, until the burning in their lungs was gone.

"Th – thank you," said Alder. "I was stuck ... I thought I was ..." He shook his head. "Oh, that was horrible."

Willow said nothing, but held him tight. For long moments all they could do was hang there, holding one another in the space behind the waterfall. Daylight glittered through the falling water. Even here, even now, it looked beautiful.

But then Willow said, "We'll have to go back through. It's the only way home."

Alder closed his eyes. He nodded, once. "All right."

Together, they dived back down through the waterfall. But this time it was easy. The water carried them down almost gently, and then tossed them back up the other side. Willow and Alder broke the surface, far from the waterfall.

And there was Fern, waiting on the bank, looking anxious and relieved all at the same time.

Chapter 7
The Great River

Willow half-pushed, half-pulled Alder to the shore. When he was safe she let him go, and grabbed the grasses at the bank edge. Her legs were heavy and cold, and it took everything she had just to drag herself from the water. Alder slipped and stumbled on the mud. Fern grabbed him by his fur, and pulled him up on to the land.

"Th – thanks," said Alder. He was trembling. His chest quivered and his paws shook. Willow huddled against him until his shaking stopped.

"Are you both all right?" said Fern.

Willow blinked up at her face. Then she nodded. "We're OK."

"I'm glad," said Fern with a smile, "but you're still cold and tired. Wait here."

Willow heard a splash, and Fern was gone. Willow half-wondered what she was doing. But nothing really mattered now, except that Alder was safe. She closed her eyes and curled tighter against her brother. But then Willow heard a rustle and a cracking noise, and felt a paw on her shoulder.

"Here, eat this," said Fern. "It'll help. You need the strength."

Fern held out a large chunk of crayfish meat. Alder staggered to his feet, and took some. He nibbled on the white flesh. Willow took some too. She swallowed the first bit, then ate the rest, ravenously. When she was done she felt a bit better.

"Where did you get that crayfish?" said Willow.

Fern smiled. "The trick is to know the easy places, the ones where you don't have to half-drown yourselves to catch one." The smile left Fern's face. "And that's why I told you not to."

"You think we were stupid, don't you?" said Alder.

Fern put her head on one side. "I think you're a fine pair of young water voles," she said. "But the truth is you were lucky. The Great River could have done a lot worse, if she had wanted to."

"Worse?" said Alder.

"Yes." Fern turned so they could see her stump of a tail. "Worse. I once lost nearly everything to her." Then Fern sighed. "She was testing you, that's all. I told you that you should give her respect. And now you know why."

Willow remembered the silly rhyme she had sung before she had swum down the rapids. She remembered the river's voice, how powerful it had sounded, how angry. She hung her head.

"Anyway, you're safe," said Fern. "You passed the Great River's test and you're back on your feet." She smiled at Willow and Alder. "And now, if you're up to it, you'd better get back to your mother. She'll be worried about you." Fern hesitated. "And maybe don't tell her too much about your adventure today. There's no harm done, and I'm sure you've both learned a lesson. There are some things that mothers don't need to know."

Fern smiled at them both. And then with a rustle she was gone.

Alder and Willow stared at each other. Willow didn't know what to say.

"I'm sorry," she said. "You told me not to insult the river. I made her angry."

Alder cleared his throat. "It's not your fault. I was the one who went back for the crayfish. If you hadn't saved me ..." He did not finish what he was saying.

"It's OK," said Willow. "We're both OK." She felt tears sting in her eyes. She brushed them away.

A half-smile spread across Alder's face. "I don't think I'll be catching crayfish any time soon," he said. "They don't taste that good anyway."

Willow hit him on the shoulder. "You are *such* a liar. They're delicious," she said. Then she smiled. "But no, I won't try catching them either."

"Good," said Alder. "Come on, let's get back to the nest."

Together, they stumbled up through the grasses. Willow was so tired that even walking hurt. But soon enough they came to the entrance to the burrow.

"Remember," said Alder. "Don't tell Mother."

"Do I look stupid?" said Willow.

Alder grinned. "Do you really want me to answer that?"

He staggered off down the tunnel, heading for the nest. Willow, though, lingered outside. Something made her want to stop, to think. She turned to face the Great River. She listened to the water. The rain had stopped, and the river sounded normal again, like she always had.

Willow walked the few
steps to the water's edge.
She put her nose down to the
shallows, until her whiskers were
almost touching the surface.
"Thank you," she whispered.
"Thank you for giving him back."
And just for a moment the sound
of the river changed. A tiny singing
noise rose from the water. There were
no words, but Willow thought she
understood. She had given the Great
River respect, and the river approved.
Willow nodded, once. Then she
turned and ran back to her burrow,
back to where it was safe and warm.

About the author

My novels *The River Singers* and *The Rising* are both about water voles, the same animals that you will find in this book. This isn't an accident! In fact, I wrote *The Crayfish Catchers* because I always felt there was a story that I had left out, one that needed telling. And now you've read it you know something nobody else does: you know what happened in the time between those books, when nobody was watching …